JOAN COLVIN

NATURE'S studio

A QUILTER'S GUIDE TO PLAYING WITH FABRICS & TECHNIQUES

C&T PUBLISHING

Text © 2005 Joan Colvin

Artwork © 2005 C&T Publishing

Publisher: Amy Marson

Editorial Director: Gailen Runge

Acquisitions Editor: Jan Grigsby

Editor: Liz Aneloski

Technical Editor: Carolyn Aune

Copyeditor/Proofreader: Stacy Chamness, Wordfirm Inc.

Cover Designer: Krisen Yenche

Design Director/Book Designer: Rose Sheifer

Illustrator: Joan Colvin

Production Assistant: Tim Manibusan

Photography: Luke Mulks and Diane Pedersen unless otherwise noted

Published by C&T Publishing, Inc., P.O. Box 1456,
Lafayette, California, 94549

Front cover: *Leafed Madrona,* page 30; *Madrona #8: Rose Sunset* page 31; *Copper, Bronze, and Gilty Pleasures,* page 35; *Unknown Bird,* page 51.
Back cover: *Crow, and Western Mountains*

Library of Congress Cataloging-in-Publication Data

Colvin, Joan
   Nature's studio : a quilter's guide to playing with fabric & techniques / Joan Colvin.
      p. cm.
   Includes index.
   ISBN 1-57120-292-7 (paper trade)
   1. Quilts--Design. 2. Quilting. I. Title.

TT835.C6478 2005   746.46--dc22

2004024709

Printed in China
10 9 8 7 6 5 4 3

Acknowledgments

Loving and grateful thanks to my husband, Bill, for his loyal patience, and to our children Scott and Amy, Annie and Todd, and Ellen and Daren for help of all kinds. Welcome insights came from my sister, Judy, and from Frank and Anne.

Thank you to my students, who amaze me with their desire to experiment. I hope you've found some independence. Finishing isn't really the point, is it? Finding something you want to finish is.

Thanks to every one of my patrons who have purchased my pieces. Though the eclectic assortment of work in this book may not include your piece, please believe I love equally well everything I've done. (Except one. Under my bed. Which you'll never see.)

Thanks to the curators and galleries that make our work accessible. And thanks to the producers of quilting seminars and events that draw us together.

Thanks to my photographers and to the very special staff at C&T, who have been superb at every point. Liz Aneloski, especially, has made this a pleasurable process for me.

Contents

1

Introduction

I'm still here, my friends. I am wandering through the world of fabric art, learning equally from my successes and from my mishaps.

I suspect many of you are doing the same. We are drawn to quilting by the fabric, the variety of choices, and the variety of methods for joining them. We are drawn by the chance to be with interesting people who are doing the same thing. Classes cover any and all aspects of the field. Large groups and small groups come together socially, helpful and supportive as you make things to show them. Quilt shops are centers of activity, like the old inns or alehouses. And galleries are more willing to open their resources to fabric art. It's all gotten quite large and impressive in the last few years, hasn't it?

So, have you found where you fit in?

I'm never sure about this. If I were new to quiltmaking and fiber art, I think I might be intimidated. The stores have such an enormous array of books. To be good at this kind of sewing, do you need to have read all of them? Or, if you are the inventive sort, you might wonder if there is anything else to say on the subject. What could you possibly contribute? Either way it can seem worrisome.

But remember, at the library you pick different books at different times to suit your tastes of the moment. At least one is just right. You need to trust that your instincts will keep you reading only what interests you. Also, trust that your own solutions to sewing issues may be just the best ones ever invented. Only so much preparation for work is useful, then you need to get into the project and learn on the job.

Your Way, My Way, Whatever Works

This book is meant to help you find your own way. Even if you have already done so, it is never a mistake to view your own work and your own working process from another angle. You will see my pieces and hear some thoughts on how they evolved. Along the way, any useful procedures will be illustrated.

I will tell you what works for me and why. If you can use any of this in your own progression, I would be delighted. I think that following my thought process on specific pieces will help you see issues. I would certainly hope that you don't have to like my personal choices to find this book useful.

Sometimes, just discovering what you don't want to do brings quiet relief.

Expressing Yourself

It's a human impulse to make art and then to want to share it. I think all of us are more willing these days to recognize the need for art in our lives. I'm surprised to find in my classes, doctors, executives, mothers of large families, helicopter pilots—people in high-stress jobs who need something they can lose themselves in.

Over the years, we have gotten more appreciative of the vast number of approaches to art, and more tolerant of the diverse materials and techniques used. We invent new substances hourly and find fresh things to say, or fresh ways to say old things.

Let's go back to the human impulse to collect beautiful or interesting things—colored petals, shiny rocks. Sorting, stacking, arranging, drawing with fingers or toes in the sand . . . the heart of the creative process. Remember how it feels?

You find that you wish to share your pleasure with someone. See what I made? Isn't it beautiful? Do you understand it? Now, sharing requires preserving or re-creating—sticking the petals onto leaves with pitch, stringing the beads, chipping into stone. And many artists feel the process isn't complete until preserving and sharing has taken place.

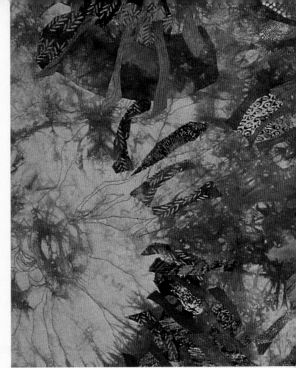

Detail of *Sea Blooms*

That first passionate part of your impulse can vary from joy and contentment to anger or angst. The second part, the sharing, involves endless variety in engineering to get your art ready to show. So really, finding your voice is reaching some sort of balance between the passion to make something and the technical requirements of doing so.

What makes this all so exciting is how absolutely infinite the choices are. How intensely do you see, how deeply do you feel, how amusing or ironic is life to you, how awesome is the visible and invisible universe? How you find your way among all this is how you speak to the world through your work. You can define yourself this way, if you wish. During the time you have alone with your work, you can make all the choices—every single one. You choose how you want to spend your time and what you want to spend it saying.

That's Why I Chose Fabric

What is joyful, what delights me about fabric composition is that colored and textured fabrics have their own symbolism. Though they may speak in different contexts, they lie in wait for me to find their meaning and voice through juxtaposition. A fabric glows and vibrates. If I can stay out of its way, give it what it needs to speak, nudge it here and there, and release it to perform, then I am an eager observer, a happy participant, and a pleasantly surprised viewer of the final outcome. Because I love literature and the stories of life, and because I never read the last line first, this method of working suits me and engages my attention to the very end. How will it all come out?

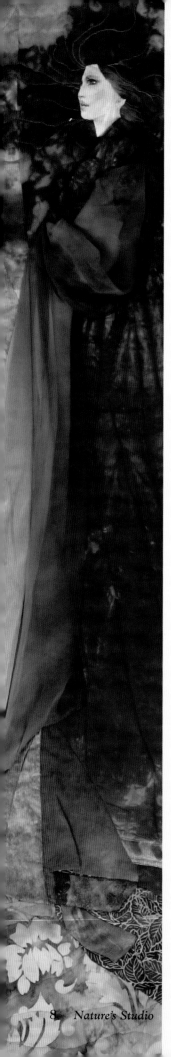

It wasn't always so clear to me that the fabric was in charge. When I first encountered the organized quilting world, I was awash in geometric abstractions. I loved it, and I questioned no aspect of it—and I still don't. It is simply wonderful. But what happened to me was unexpected. My fingers needed to feel and pull and play with this medium rather like one would mold clay. I began to think of brush strokes and meandering lines. I truly considered going back to paper and canvas. But never underestimate the raw power of a piece of fabric: it shimmers, it folds, it does everything but whistle. I couldn't leave fabric. I moved from geometric piecing to hand and machine appliquéing quilt tops. Now I swiftly apply fabric onto a previously prepared backing and batting sandwich (which I call my "canvas"). My huge brushstrokes of colored fabric have hard and soft edges as they would in painting, and I have found what is to me an utterly free process that is open to endless possibility.

A Word on Style

It's not a given that you will be choosing an object to replicate in some way. In fact, you may start with a hazy, abstract idea to which no images are yet attached. In dream sequences, objects do appear and they can be symbolic of fairly amorphous concepts. But if you are making art with fabric, something ultimately needs to be cut and sewed.

Real-life shapes may be stylized to make a point. That is what graphic art is all about. I've always believed that knowledge gained from intense scrutiny of a shape (taking in all the details, understanding how they fit, why they are there—all this) tends to deepen your respect for the subject and strengthen your ability to make good choices. First, see reality very clearly. Then choose symbols, simplify, and summarize down to what you feel is the essence. This will require some further thinking as you go along.

But how do we account for the freshness of a child's painting? It is an innocent abstraction. Without much knowledge, a child zeros in straight to the heart, with clarity and laserlike accuracy. It's breathtaking. "Go figure," as they say.

I'd like to believe that not only are we born with this ability to see, and to see through and beyond, but that this ability is still there, just a bit hammered and trampled. Given a bit of quiet, you might find clarity again. Some shaking and airing out might help.

2

Recognizable Style

What Is a Recognizable Style?

The word "style" is tricky. There is a difference between style of work (the character of the images you make) and style of working (the procedures you use to get there). We will be discussing the former, the look of your work. Yet, at the end you will know better how to structure the latter. *After* you have thought about what you are trying to achieve, you may wish to refer to my working process for help in structuring your own (see Chapter 9, page 72).

So what is a recognizable style? It means just what it says, that when people see your work, they can identify it as yours. Your own particular choices fit into a pattern that is becoming consistent, and you are sufficiently comfortable with this set of choices that you can settle in to work more deeply and more searchingly within the framework you've chosen.

That makes sense to me. Personally, I'm more intrigued by the set of choices I've made than I am by whether my work is recognized as mine.

Are You Ready to Develop a Style of Your Own? What Do You Like Doing Best with Fabric?

We are enticed into working with fabric in so many ways, for so many reasons. Many of us have tried, or are trying, everything. We take classes, we do group projects, we get the feel for what is available throughout the vast world of fabric construction. We do it all. This is great fun and very satisfying.

If you've been around for a while, however, or if you've experienced being an artist in other media, you may sense a need for more. It just happens at some point that you want to have a more serious relationship with your fabric. There are many clues. Among them, you begin to have a sense of what you like doing best with fabric, and you notice that you've been avoiding other choices. You may begin to feel restless with patterns or in classes. Your friends aren't surprised when your work is a little different. They begin to have expectations for what they might see in your work. You work intensely, and it isn't enough—there is more to say. You work in a series, and there is *still* more to say. Some part of what you are doing is irresistible, and the challenge to get it "right" (so you like it and can leave it) doesn't go away.

Notice that I've not mentioned the need for any particular *skill* level. Learning the "how-to" can come at any time, and you may even make up your own procedures. The answers come as you immerse yourself in more and more fabric projects—you learn with each piece you do.

What I have spoken of is an inner sense that says, "Yeah, I love this. I want to do it whenever I have a choice. I want to find out what will happen if I . . ."

If you experience this, you might be ready to see if you have a style of your own—a way of speaking through fabric that feels right to you and becomes identifiably yours.

Viewer's Impression

When you first glance at a painting or other work of art, you have instant impressions. Perhaps you respond to color first, or notice the absence of color. Perhaps you respond to the mood—lifelike or romantic or unpleasant. You could be fascinated with the uniqueness of the assemblage—How does it stay together? How was this fastened to that? You might be touched by the delicacy and intricacy of a tiny piece or be overwhelmed and awed by the hugeness of something towering before you. I could go on and on. Much of the time, though, there is little need to analyze or identify these things—naming a response doesn't add or detract from my own viewing experience. But if you enjoy having the ability to discuss and critique artworks, there is a world of formal learning out there to guide you.

As a producer of fabric pieces, though, you may be very interested in what leads to these various impressions. If we talk a little about the choices you face, you will see how many you make easily and instinctively; you may also get help with some less obvious choices. You will see which choices are most important to you—and which areas do not interest you in the least. Developing a style means selecting and internalizing a set of choices that become your signature way of working.

Lines, Spaces, and How They Join

Line: Straight or Curved

"I can't draw a straight line," you may say. But you can make one with a ruler or with the computer; and it could go on forever, without curving unless some outside pull or force affects it. I'm imagining the line needed to target another planet—straight, really, but pulled by gravity into curves. It's beyond my comprehension. I am more comfortable with the lines of nature that I can see. These lines are twisted and turned by every outside force you can envision—changes of the seasons, pressures, rainfall, and so on. I love the undulating lines that represent growing, changing, and developing. Though we all use both straight and curved lines, you will be drawn to one more than the other. Just notice.

Spaces: Geometric or Organic

As you draw two lines, the relationship between them begins to form a space. Whether the lines are straight ruled or undulating (organic), the areas between them take on shapes.

Put another way, a shape stops at an edge; these edges determine how big and how complicated the shape becomes. For the fun of it, visualize a child's coloring book in which shapes are formed with simple hard lines. Then, in contrast, picture an upturned paint bucket with paint slowly oozing out over a surface—where are the edges to contain the paint? Perhaps a little surface tension and drying capacity will slow it down, perhaps some invisible activity at the edge, some tiny line developing. Let space come alive in your mind—spaces that you can allow to ebb and flow, or neatly corral and cut off.

Joining Lines and Spaces

Well, the lines and spaces are already joined, aren't they? We can focus on one or the other, but where line stops, space begins, and vice versa. The "joining" lines may be thin or thick. *Straight joinings* make geometric shapes— rectangles, triangles. *Curved joinings* can be precise, using the arcs of geometry, or undulating and organic. Already, other combinations and variations are no doubt occurring to you.

Quality of Lines and Spaces: Hard Edge or Soft Edge

Remember the feel of a paintbrush? As it comes out of the paint pot full of liquid color and you begin to pull it over the surface, you get a clear, neat (what I call *hard-edge*) line. But as you use up the paint, the line begins to feather out, the paper shows through, and you are now making what I call a *soft-edge* line. And, of course, while making the lines, you are making spaces beside them of the same quality. So, now another choice for you: in addition to thick or thin and straight or curved, your lines and shapes can be hard or soft edged. As in painting, you can use one or the other, or both in the same piece.

Assembling Lines and Spaces: Techniques for Producing Edges

We've just said lines and spaces are joined. That's easy to see in a pencil drawing. The painter draws a brush over a surface, and that is the assembly process. The artist whose material is yellow hazelnut pollen spreads it in geometric shapes and mounds across a surface; careful spreading is his assembly process. We in quiltmaking get to figure out how we will form fabric and thread into lines and spaces—and we have many different assembly processes. We'll look at some now.

Detail of *Natural Spot Light,* page 39. The relationship between lines begins to form shapes.

HARD EDGE

A hard edge looks crisp, neat, and clean, like the polished tile in a palace floor. The checkerboard is a beloved, livable fixture of civilization. Hard edges are obtained easily in fabric by a <u>simple</u> <u>seam</u> that, when opened up, has joined two shapes, side by side. Even if the fabric is the same color, a tiny crisp seamline may still be visible. Carefully turned <u>appliqué</u> gives the same effect—a neat hard edge.

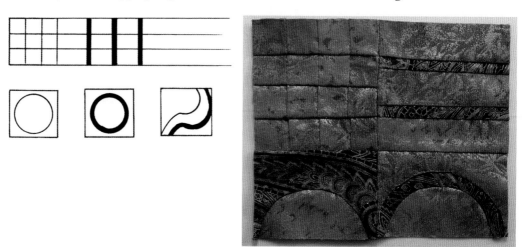

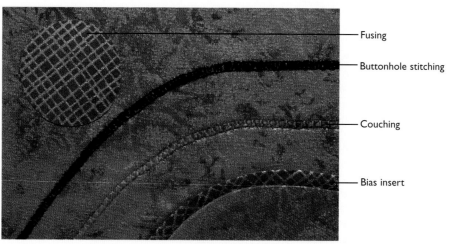

Hard-edged piecing

You can see that there will be many combinations of these crisp, neat choices. And, indeed, any set of templates in irregular shapes joined together, either abutting or with sashing or other lines between, is a combination of the above elements.

The hard edges discussed above are produced by <u>traditional piecing methods</u>. Other ways to produce these effects could include various applications to the surface—<u>fusing</u> of stabilized fabric, for one. Fused edges can be absolutely neat, the effect of one fabric beside another. If a thicker line is desired, <u>bias tape</u> or a <u>bias insert</u> can be used. <u>Couching</u> is firm looking, too. Or, a tight <u>satin stitch</u> or <u>buttonhole stitch</u> can thicken the outer edge evenly. I'm reminded of Jane Sassaman's use of strong finishing lines to produce strength and power. You may think of further examples of externally applied hard edges.

Fusing

Buttonhole stitching

Couching

Bias insert

Hard-edge surface applications

Look through a book of famous paintings. Imagine yourself in the studios of the artists who created these works, surrounded not with paint, brushes, and prepared surfaces, but with thread, fabric, and sewing devices. How would you put things together to get these results? Look very carefully at the joinings and the quality of lines.

SOFT EDGE

So how do we get the feathered look of the almost empty paintbrush? Normal seaming doesn't do it automatically. <u>Raw-edge appliqué</u> done by hand or machine is the simplest way. Keeping in mind the rough look of torn paper, you can cut irregular edges in the fabric and then stitch them down using a <u>straight stitch</u> or a very <u>narrow zigzag stitch</u>. The viewer sees one fabric shape butted up to another fabric shape, producing a shared soft line. Technically, we do not care which is actually on top—from normal viewing distance the effect is the same.

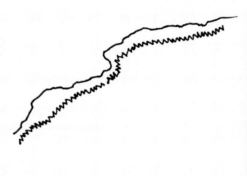

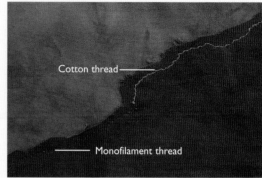

Cotton thread

Monofilament thread

Raw-edge appliqué

An even rougher edge might require a bit of <u>raveling.</u> It is easiest to stitch the fabric, then ravel it back to the stitching. Very loose raveling, almost <u>fringing,</u> can be stitched down where needed—neatly like basketry, or haphazardly like a haystack.

Raveling and fringing

You can <u>singe</u> the edges of fabrics that melt; the tiny gummy residue stops the fraying action while producing a lovely curl or a gentle organic irregular edge.

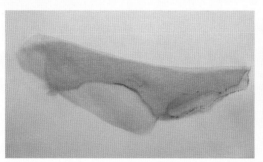

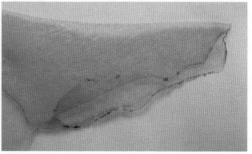

Singed edges

An even softer line that fades in and out can be obtained by using sheer fabrics, layering as much as you wish. Using <u>overlapping sheers</u>, you have enormous control over the strength of the line—like adding water to paint. Experiment with bonding agents or fray sealants. If total transparency is required, you may not even want appliqué thread to show, so random, <u>loose tacking with monofilament thread </u>affords the best chance of invisibility.

Overlapping sheer fabrics

Now, view a soft line as one that has the pebbly look of a crayon. To re-create this look, I like <u>inserts</u>. A painter may leave white spaces on purpose, missing some places on the canvas as color is roughly filled in. In quilting, insert a tiny piece of light fabric when you need this effect, as if you really were covering up little places where your batting shows through. Sometimes this is just the line-softening device needed.

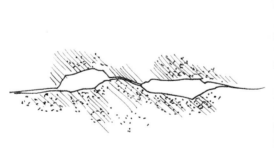

Inserts to break or soften a line

Or, find a piece of fabric in the colors you are using that is actually textured or pebbly. Insert a strip. The pebbly dots will combine with the more solid color and the joining lines will be less obvious than the new, soft lines wiggling between colors.

Insert transition fabric

Now think of soft lines as cracks between rocks. Using the same insert technique, appliqué irregular (hard- or soft-edged) rock shapes on top of the insert, which becomes the crack—behind the rocks, wonderful soft lines have developed. In the same way, inserts can be used effectively as colored edges, a halo effect, or the effect of standing under neon lights.

I often hear my students say, "I'll soften the edges with <u>embroidery</u> later." Yes, of course, the <u>threadwork</u> on top can soften edges and produce meandering lines. (Do realize, though, that if you are planning extensive threadwork and/or <u>machine embroidery</u>, this may become a design element more than a line softener.)

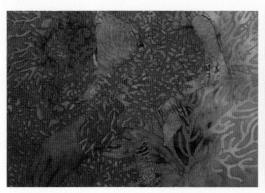 

Inserts as colored edges

HARD AND SOFT COMBINATIONS

If you are still with me, I wonder if you are getting a little muddled, wondering whether hard edges can go in undulating lines or whether soft edges can go perfectly straight. It is easy to get mixed up here. It's not as if we *have* to separate or label. But it is important that we see how this all interrelates, and how we can mix and match these components to come up with a procedure that we like to do and that gives us the flexibility to make our own statements. So let's take a moment to see some useful and effective combinations of what we've already discussed.

Combining Hard and Soft Edges: During machine appliqué, turn under those edges you want hard and leave ragged those you want soft. This is probably my favorite technique. When doing the soft part, your appliqué stitch will need to come inside ⅛" to ¼" in order to hold (see the raw-edge appliqué illustration, page 13).

Disappearing Hard Edge: This is another favorite. Let the fabric pattern determine the quality of line. That is, a hard seamline will quite delicately disappear in the confusion of strong texture or pattern. Remember that similar values or colors will melt together when viewed from a distance. The new visual line you want will be made this way—the new line will emerge in the pattern, totally unrelated to where seams are. (This concept is behind the disappearing grid of some watercolor quilts.)

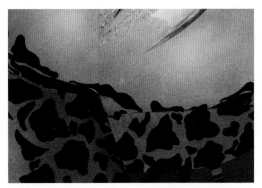 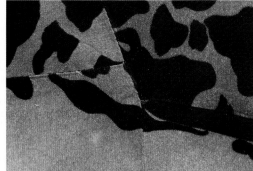

Disappearing hard edge

Detail of *Women of Cloth*, page 63

Mosaic Method: Making cracks appear by appliquéing irregularly over an insert results in a natural look. But the same method used less haphazardly can look architectural. Think of grout between mosaics, brickwork, or stone walls. Think shingles (more overlap) or adobe. As you straighten and square up the appliquéd pieces, you may find that you could just as well be doing geometric piecing. But, you'll lose the opportunity to skew one or two, or change color or size later in your composition. (Finished stitching is harder to modify later.) A compromise might be to swiftly piece, then appliqué some irregular pieces on top, here and there.

Bargello: (Soft line appears while using hard-edge style.) Hard, straight-ruled <u>strip piecing</u> can yield moving lines within. Either the stitch joints (which no longer meet) draw your eye along, or pattern and color in the fabric do it. You can let this happen randomly, or you can plan it. This is exactly what we love about bargello—the movement and life that emerge when edges no longer meet precisely.

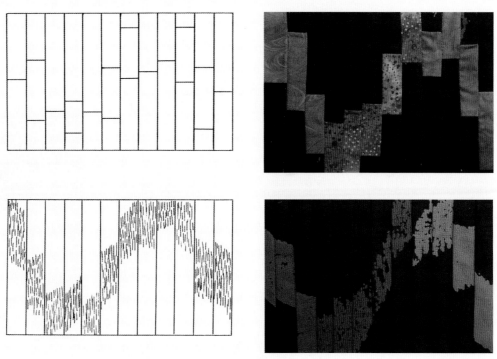

Bargello

Detail of *Who Are We This Time?*, page 62

Caterpillars: This is the name I've given to a softened, smaller, more flexible version of the bargello on page 17. It is a nice bridge between the crispness of traditional piecing and a more relaxed, collagelike approach. Little irregular scraps are stitched together (hard edge) to make clumps; these clumps have interesting top and bottom edges, all uneven (soft). And by leaving ¼" open at the beginning and end of the seaming, there is the possibility of twisting and easing, like the movements of a caterpillar. So you have little prestitched, "premixed" clumps to use in collagelike appliqué. It's like mixing your colors and experimenting a little before you paint. Your strokes take whatever shape you choose—from the chunks of Cubism to the airiness of Alexander Calder.

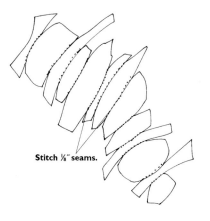

Stitch ⅛" seams.

Construction of caterpillars: Right sides together, sew ⅛" seams. Start and stop-stitching ¼" from edges. May be pressed open on back or eased while pressing.

Detail of *Sea Blooms*,
photo by Hazel A. Hynds

Pin Tucks: You can make neat, ruled, straight pin tucks, but even so, you will get a little movement as they appear to try to lie flat. To get even more movement, make your pin tucks randomly spaced. Make an effort to stitch most of them on the bias. Their natural twisting may give you some shadows and other soft effects. Even if your stitching is perfectly straight along the edge, the twisting and shadowing change the *appearance* of the spaces and widths.

Detail of pin tucks in *Heron Illusion*,
page 47

Weaving: Notice that fabric strips of uniform width can crush and crowd when woven, forming little shadows and pockets and other irregularities.

Detail of *Fanfare*, page 57

QUILTING

There are two things to remember about quilting: you have a chance to add external lines, and you have a chance to form subtle new shapes as the quilting makes new edges. Just realize that it is another chance to incorporate line and shape into your work. I view a quilting line as that point when the artist comes in with pen or brush to add finishing details, strengthen lines, lay in delicate tracery, and otherwise underline or complete areas. (Also. realize that you can use quilting as a textural or embroidery device, such as stitching all over a small piece, then appliquéing it onto a larger work. This is not usage of line the way we are discussing it here, but remember this possibility when we discuss texture, page 21.)

So, just as you have made other choices, you must make quilting-line choices—they will become part of your style. These lines can be straight or evenly curved or meandering. Various weights of thread can give you fine, medium, or very thick lines. In relationship to each other, these lines can be evenly spaced or clustered and massed. (For example, many parallel and overlapping thin lines can produce a thick line.) In relation to the total piece, they can be spaced evenly throughout or clustered in certain areas.

Note, too, that the *absence* of traditional quilting lines will make a statement. Many quilters use <u>hand stitching</u> of all sorts to fasten through the layers.

Besides adding lines, the quilting affects shapes. Consider the thick oil paintings of van Gogh. Viewed sideways, the surface of his canvas is not flat. Ours in quilting isn't either, unless we choose that. Dense quilting will keep the surface flat. Less dense quilting forms pockets that create three-dimensional effects. Using <u>trapunto</u> (a technique for stuffing quilted spaces) will exaggerate that. Also affecting the dimension is the type of batting you choose. Some quilters want no puffiness, and substitute something flatter than batting. Your choices of batting, stitching density, and thickness of thread affect the size and quality of these subtle additional shapes.

The Next Step: Fitting This All Together

So, you have some choice in the matter of tools. You are ready to go on to the next set of choices: What kinds of lines and shapes do you like? How big? How many? Where? What colors? How strong? What more do you need to know?

I hope you are becoming more observant, more able to see forms and objects as combinations of line and shape. Good. Now we need a very swift overview of some other concepts that may help you along.

Subject Matter

Artists can also be defined by their choice of subject matter. What you see from the porch rocking chair. What you would like to travel to see. Mystical imagery no one else can see. Perhaps you are not "looking," but you are thinking or feeling—doing narrative work, or abstract concepts not based on visual images. Whether you choose to do a little of everything or zoom in on one topic for life, this choice is a big one. It's big because it's pretty much the reason you are doing art. You have something to say, something that wants to come out. And whatever objects or symbols you choose to make this happen will be important to you and will help transmit your sense of the world to viewers.

I include under "subject matter" any preparation or research you need. What do you already know? What aspects are most interesting? Immerse yourself in the subject until your ideas are ready to burst forth.

Design or Composition

Composition can be based on *repetition* of one form—the heart of our quilting tradition. The forms may be *turned, reversed, tessellated,* or *varied in size.* Repetition is a tried and true way to get unity and balance.

Detail of *A Valley Loved*, private collection, photo by Hazel A. Hynds. Want to repeat a shape, but you can't find the right fabric? Try a potato block to print the shape you want onto the fabric. Though there are many commercial substances for carving blocks, potatoes are easy. If you think they will shrivel up before you are through stamping, you can plan to make several potato blocks the same shape. For *A Valley Loved*, I had found large white tulips in fabric, but none of the medium lavender tulips I needed.

If the subject matter doesn't lend itself to repetition, then you must create some relationships. There could still be subtle repetition of some portions of the object, or of background spaces. Vary the size of your spaces. Let some shapes *point* or *lead* into others (not off the edge!) so that the eye swirls around within the structure. Space around an object gives it room to breathe—serenity. Crowding creates tension.

Cropping is a word that describes selecting, framing, and/or cutting out only the part of the design you want to use—a most useful process. You can zoom in or out, as you would with a camera.

Depth, Perspective, Light, and Shadow

You'll need to consider whether your lines and shapes are to be flat (like some stained-glass windows or rugs)—that is, one-dimensional.

The moment you vary the value or color within a shape—that is, let some parts of it be lighter or darker or different—you begin to see dimension or depth, or *shading*, as we call it. Basic drawing classes help you observe what happens when light falls on an object, creating shadows.

As you move farther away from the object, you may need to understand perspective (the yellow line down the highway disappearing at a distant point on the horizon). The objects in your foreground may appear larger and more (or less) textured than the mid-distance objects. As in camera work, you may set your focus where you wish—foreground fuzzy or background fuzzy. Your choice.

As you can see, what you do within and around your shapes affects their roundness and their realness.

Value

I suggested that things begin to happen when you make parts lighter or darker. Oh, yes. *Value* is a powerful tool. Value is simply the scale from black through all the grays to white. (And, in color, all the way from lightest to darkest.) When I say "blackout," or "whiteout," you see the potential, don't you? You have total control over what the viewer *sees*—the object hidden in background shadows, sun lighting up a face . . . Think of Rembrandt, who was a master of using light. Value can be changed by increasing not only the intensity of the color but also the density of the textural detail. (Imagine increasing layers of netting.) A photocopy in black and white will help you see contrasts. Try a copy of a photocopy!

Texture

Texture is what we feel with our fingers, the tactile experience. We in fabric think of *texture* as plain, shiny, ribbed, furry, or velvety, and we may notice whether the thread count is high or low. We can do things with fabric that painters can only dream about—they have to replicate or *suggest* texture by density of line, pattern, and shadow, all in one dimension. If we use smooth cotton fabric that has been *printed*

with pattern, we, like painters, are working with one-dimensional surfaces that have been "drawn on" to replicate those real textures. We have a great deal more latitude in choosing visual textures.

Use an instant or digital camera as you work. Hand-dyes, more than regular fabrics, sneak up on you—they swirl around and form unexpectedly dimensional shapes.

Many quilters produce their own textural surfaces with hand and machine work; that is, they make their own fabric texturally thickened with thread and other media.

Color

I want to be sure you appreciate that color comes from light—color in all its splendor and intensity. Light bounces off objects, coloring them, too. There is so much written about color. Personally, I don't worry about the physics of light entering my retina; I just want to know what to grab when I'm working.

You need to be able to separate the clear colors of the rainbow from the mixtures of shades and tones that produce a less pure, less saturated, earthier color. Tea-dying changes white to off-white or oatmeal to blend in with the more subdued colors. You will no doubt find that you like one color group better than the other. (My preference is oatmeal; I accept that.) There is no good or bad—it's just that the two groups don't always mix well. The intense clear colors of the rainbow overwhelm the more subdued colors, which become muddy by contrast. Sort your fabrics accordingly. Treasure those that fit in both groups and can serve as transitions.

Mood and Atmosphere

The quality of light coming in your window changes, and its brightness or gloominess affects your mood. Here is another powerful tool that will help you express your ideas and feelings. In bright blue light, you can see echoes of blue on light objects; under overcast skies, there is less contrast in value, less color.

If you are working in flat pattern or some other stylized way, light may not be an issue. (Now is a good time to say that when I use the word "stylized" I am describing choices that do not adhere exactly to the old rules of drawing and painting based on photographic replication of objects. So, this word "stylized" covers every other approach that you can think of—commercial art, Asian woodcuts, the work of Grandma Moses. That is why I say light may not be an issue in these cases.)

So, what else establishes mood? Rounded, curving lines evoke different images than angular or architectural lines do. Flowery fabric seems different from stripes or plaids. My students have heard me say, "You wouldn't normally use large tropical prints for a twelfth-century monastery." Someone told me that each piece of fabric comes with its own baggage, its own symbol. Even something very specific like a printed animal can say more . . . Hand-processed African fabric? Batik? Cheap cotton, mass-produced for children's clothing? Photoprint? You will get better and better at identifying what *effect* each fabric produces. What does it bring to the party?

Size and Shape of Your Finished Piece

Are you a miniaturist or a Velda Newman? Size and shape can define an artist. These choices become a signature way of working. Most of us are in the middle somewhere, and our work takes on a size more or less as a result of other decisions. Have you tried letting size dictate your design? It's a refreshing exercise.

You will see many more pieces hanging on exhibition walls that make their statement primarily by being strange, irregular shapes, in one or more parts.

A Style of Your Own

Finding your own style is fitting it all together. I'm guessing that you were interested in or connected with some parts of this chapter and that you skimmed over others. That is exactly right—your final "selection" system depends on listening to yourself and noticing the intensity of your interest. Some of you will have already invented other choices. Good. Still, you can read about these components and feel you understand, but when you are facing your design wall, it's not so clear. What will I do first? Where do I start?

In the following sections detailing my own pieces, I will share some of my thoughts. I think there is value in following along, even if you work very differently. You will be making decisions vicariously, putting your own spin on everything . . . "Why did she . . . ? I would have . . ." Some of this constant choice making is so intrinsic, so much instinct, that you won't need to name it, and that is what you hope will occur more easily with each piece you produce.

Detail of *Great Aunt Jenny*, page 67

"In and Out" Process

My style is a kind of realism. I do not assume you will want to work the way I do. Consider this: If you have some large, simple, colored shapes before you, and they are gorgeous as is, you may wish to fasten them down as a wonderful abstraction. If a group of fabrics gets you thinking of something in the known world, and a little bit of detail will show this (that is, direct the viewer to the same conclusion), then your work becomes less abstract. Or the shapes may become recognizable but not in the usual context (symbolism). As the shapes gain more definition, the options for assigning meaning to them become narrower, and you can see how we get to realism or representational art. Should you get even realer than real, I call that surrealism.

Now, we can work backward, too. Beginning with real objects or ideas, placing them in settings, removing detail, simplifying shapes, seeing essences—here we come all the way back to the beautiful simple shapes I first mentioned. Nobody but you cares where you begin or end. I call this the "in and out" process—it is a record of the mental and/or visual focus, and it can swell in and out like deep breathing . . . For the purposes of this book, I am beginning with real things, because that's what I do. You will be able to work in or out from these.

Choosing a Familiar Subject to Begin

I don't much like the word "start." It's like startle, or the start of a race, or off to a slow start, or, worst, the word before you begin a horrible test. I prefer easing into things, so my momentum is underway before I realize I'm on the path. That is what we will do here. We won't "start." We will watch something wonderful and sort and choose fabrics to express this. You will see as we go along how chunks of fabric can be used directly on the surface. Somewhere along the way, a photograph or simple sketch might be useful to find out how something fits or to help determine value or placement. A good shape, to be repeated, may require you to make a template. These tools will be a natural solution to issues as they arise, and as you make choices.

For the purposes of this book, let's have the beginning be a love affair with your subject, whatever it may be.

Our subject will stay the same; all other components may vary. I like to create trees, because we all know them intimately, and there are so many species, which allows us enormous variation—even more as we venture into the magical. (Just realize that much of what we say about trees—and later birds and bodies—can be used for most other subject matter you might choose, whether that be flowers, mountains, seascapes, or less realistic images and symbols.)

Each piece we talk about will have required selecting from among the various style choices. Some issues aren't pertinent; others will be crucial. If I don't discuss color, then it wasn't key to my thinking, or it was chosen easily. I'll tell you what interested me, and I'll often suggest where divergence might have taken me. And the discussion of each piece has some little point that might help you.

5

Being With Trees

Hiding in the prune tree at my grandmother's house, leaf collecting on walks with my mother, picking huckleberries from bushes growing out of cedar stumps, picnicking while sitting in the woods on old logs or on driftwood at the beach, trying to encircle a Douglas fir with my arms . . . all my senses were engaged or I wouldn't be able to remember such long-ago pleasures. My father's early adventures as an engine wiper aboard the *President Madison* going back and forth to Japan led us to Seattle's Asian art museums—happy times staring at the brush paintings of ancient trees. I loved that in a few strong strokes the struggle of the tree to find air and water, to adapt to the wind and make its roots secure were communicated to us—me, very young;, my parents older. My concept of the hugeness of time seems entangled with the hugeness of trees.

What Do You Want to Say About Your Tree?

This question may sound a little naive, but it is among the most important I will ask. What is it (about this or any other subject you've chosen) that is holding your attention? Why are you doing a piece on this particular subject? What about it has piqued your interest?

I've just given you a tiny sample of why trees are important to me—beyond their appearance. Now we'll move to the more physical observations of trees, and my questions will relate to what you actually see. Look at the tree (and this can be entirely in your imagination, drawing on a compilation of memories, viewing an assortment of photos, or you and the tree nose to nose). What about it seems most interesting to you? Why do you care?

Is it the shape or the size? Or its adaptation to the site? Is it the texture of the bark? Or the color in daylight or at sunset? How many branches? Are they heavy or lacy? Are there leaves? Is there light behind them or on them? Where is the light coming from? Is light important to the scene? Will the trees perhaps be whimsical or fanciful so light won't be an issue? Where are they planted?

Now, in thinking about this, you are noticing your impressions. You don't need to articulate or write down your answers. You are testing yourself to see how much you have seen, how much you know, how involved you are. Depth of knowledge can help you speak.

At this point, also, you are mentally toying with how this idea could be expressed (i.e., you are sifting through those style choices, wondering which will best express this subject your way). You are essentially immersing yourself in the subject matter. How much research and immersion is enough? One day you'll just feel ready.

In telling you about my trees, I'll deal with some of these questions. The following quick samples, which I call the "Woodskin Series," will be a perfect way to ease into our arboreal experience.

Woodskin Series: A Quick Look at Treemaking

Golden Hardwood

Golden Hardwood, 21" x 41", 2002

Even easier than looking at a tree, or photographing one, is finding a piece of fabric with a tree already printed on it! Starting with what I call a *keynote* fabric—in this case, the purple and gold hardwood tree fabric in the upper right corner—made life simple. (A keynote fabric is any one that gives you an idea or seems to be a good place to begin. It doesn't have to be there to the end, nor do you have to use very much of it.)

So the characteristics of this tree were already established. Because the print was small and fuzzy, it was sufficiently ambiguous that I thought I could imagine what a larger version was supposed to look like. Had I wanted to veer off in other directions, I could have fooled the viewer into believing all sorts of different things about these little trees in the distance. But I chose the first, simplest approach that came to mind.

The composition was straightforward—place the printed tree fabric in the distance, make a tree of medium size, and finally design a really large one for the major object. This large one was pure fantasy. Of course, my idea of fantasy might be much different from yours. The little printed tree could have sent me to the tree books for more detail, but I know enough about how trees look to make up something that feels right and amuses me. In the context of the little print, something too wildly different might have been out of place. My idea was to use that print to provide a distant background. So the trees should appear to be the same species, right? Had I decided to go with an inventive vision, I might have needed to discard the original fabric. After all, it did its job, getting me going.

Color was already chosen—purple and gold, opposites on the color wheel. Adding some small gold leaves to the keynote fabric disguised the pattern repeat and added a golden glow I could use throughout to warm up the deep purple.

The trees in the keynote fabric have a soft look, like painting or a fuzzy photograph. So I chose the soft-edge assembly process that mimics this—machine appliqué using hard and soft edges, with fabric collaged over the batting and fastened down (see "Hard and Soft Combinations," page 16).

So, sorting among the choices, you see that I cared about repeated shapes in a simple composition. I accepted the given color palette. I chose an assembly method that let me express the softness and irregularity of bark in a realistic way. Line wasn't much of a design factor, was it? Just a little in the quilting to hold down the tree bark.

Oh My, Mars, 36" x 43", 1997, private collection, photo by Hazel A. Hynds. Different subject matter, but also using a keynote fabric, objects enlarged from it, variation in size, and repetition.

Aspen

Here, too, I started with a keynote fabric—a decorator piece that contained some brownish shapes on white, making me think of the "eyes" on birch or aspen. Even though the shapes varied, cutting them out and placing them where branches might connect to the trunk leads the viewer to accept that symbolic shape as natural. Quilting around these eyes, and around the trunk's diameter, gives the impression of that sort of tree—adding line as well as rounder shapes.

The brown and white color scheme was monochromatic, with high contrast in value, emphasizing the lightness we associate with this family of trees.

As to composition: I had only a few brown spots, so the traditional thick grove of trees was out. (I could have included a dense grove of distant trees, much smaller. I still might do that; I like the idea.) Three trees are better than two—the rule that an odd number of items used together is more interesting than an even number still works

Aspen, 22" x 42", 2002

for me. Squeezing two trees together is natural; they often cluster at the base. This allows some angling—a pleasant variation in the strong dark, negative space.

Assembly was the hard and soft combination, which is pretty standard for me, unless otherwise noted.

Also shown are two hard-edged variations of this color scheme. In the top example, strip piecing gives an abstract impression of birch or aspen, and fabric choices establish a strong and cheerful mood. In the bottom example, which is also hard-edge strip pieced, fabric choices more obviously evoke nature, and, moreover, they are in a scale appropriately natural to the size of the tree trunks. To help suggest depth, three background fabrics are stitched together before slicing them up for stripping with trees. These meandering horizontal lines are softening, as is the irregular bottom finish (hard-edge appliqué). With very few fabrics, mood can be established—in this case, somber.

Aspen variations

Pine

I suppose you could call the pine needle fabric the keynote fabric, but actually, it came last. I wanted to do a tree trunk using red and green (a challenge for me—as you see, red-orange and khaki is the best I could do), having been astounded to notice that the outermost bark of the pine tree explodes, leaving a reddish younger layer underneath. How could I have missed this before? So, exaggerating the color was fun. You can view the red underlayer as a very large *insert*, below.

To show the bark texture and the "twistiness" of a pine in a small composition was my plan. Because the expanding bark is naturally very rough edged, I machine quilted the pieces of bark onto the reddish layer directly. Appliqué wasn't needed.

Detail

Pine, 18" x 42", 2002

Madrona: Vision of a Favorite Tree (A Fuller Look at Process)

Madrona in Wet Meadow, 40" x 58", 1997, private collection, photo by Hazel A. Hynds

Leafed Madrona, 30" x 63", 2000, private collection

Madrona in Morning Light, 36" x 54", 1998, private collection, photo by Hazel A. Hynds

Madrona #8: Rose Sunset, 35" x 56", 2000

One of my favorite trees is the madrona, called arbutus in Canada. These trees are threatened now, but as a child, I saw them everywhere, especially when riding the ferries into the coves of Puget Sound. How could a tree trunk be orange, pink, and variations of red ochre? And how surprising is the peeled interior, opened up and silky smooth, golden chartreuse. The Northwest supplies its own very green background, whether it be the waters of the Sound or the meadows nearby.

The previous several versions of the madrona continue my affair with this tree. In each of them, I am painting, my huge brush strokes of colored fabric sweeping cleanly when strength is needed and dragging a bit raggedly where nature is less definite. In many, I've added madrona-like leaves, which have been fussy cut and subsequently quilted directly onto branches (see "Making Leaves," page 40).

Madrona #11: Soft Leather, 29" x 57", 2003, private collection

In *Madrona #11*, the enlarged trunk has become the composition. I used wrinkled pink suede as the ragged bark and added transparent reflective ribbons throughout. Knotholes have been enlarged and made fanciful. Branches of silk and other ribbons were stitched on net first to give me more choice in how they were positioned (see "Making Branches," page 36).

Detail

Sometimes I use commercial fabric as a shortcut for water. The sky and its light upon the tree and upon the water must all be compatible. To get this compatibility, pastel pencils or fabric paint can help blend in the sky or add color touches to the water.

Throughout this madrona series I'm dealing with design relationships among the trunks themselves and between the trunks and the background. Because trees are naturally graceful, it would seem easy just to wind them around the scene. But it's never that simple for me. Add in some other factors: How much of that perfect trunk fabric do you have? Do you want to cover up an improbable jog in the water? Should there be one bigger tree? Where should the others be planted? Is that branch too strong, leading the eye out of the picture? Do these trees normally grow tightly together in a thicket? Should there be multiple trunks? You can see that the more you know about your tree, the easier answers will come to you. But the little technical issues will still intervene. For example, I'm wondering on another level: if I'm using repetition of trunks for unity, are there enough of them?

When you have some tentative answers, you will have solved some light and color choices, and you will have a better feel for where these trees are located, whether or not they need leaves or branches, and even what sort of quilting will add texture. Somewhere in the midst of this you will need to decide how the tree is connected to the ground—usually the last decision I make (see "Planting the Tree," page 42).

So, when you know what you want to say and what effects you want, *there are a great number of perfectly acceptable ways to achieve this*, and you will find one you like. You just need to stay with it until you have some convictions or get a jolt of enthusiasm for your idea.

From Vision to Cutting Table

Making Trunks

How to begin? I try to position my trees first, with large hunks of the basic color. This may involve several tries and some instant camera shots to compare. Try to feel in your fingers how these trees grow—their girth, their height, and their straightness or gnarliness.

CUTTING FABRIC

I've found that cutting straight strips can be limiting. No matter which species you're doing, cutting on the bias a bit irregularly will lend life and strength and let you mold the fabric to shape. Cutting roughly with scissors, start at a corner and cut diagonally. You will leave a corner chunk that may be useful later. With a few additional cuts, any strips you don't use can be made into organic shapes.

Cutting bias strips for trees

Any fabric cut on the bias can be folded or twisted gracefully, often showing an interesting wrong side. Layering, twisting, and sculpting an assortment of fabrics in a variety of colors, textures, and scales can occupy you for a long, happy time. I'm being brief here because your imagination will take over.

FLEXIBILITY IN POSITIONING WHILE COMPOSING DESIGN

If your trunk is large and simple, only pinning the trunk will hold it in shape while allowing you to move it around in your design and slip various potential backgrounds behind it.

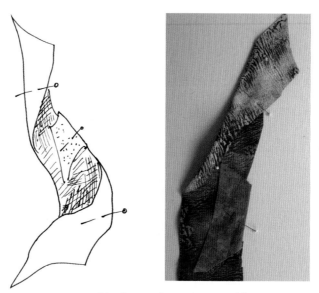

Pin the trunk so it's moveable.

As you pin on more fabric detail, these pins will add to the stability of the trunk and will hold sufficiently. I find it easier to rely on pins than to work on a backing or baste, because I may want to change the shape altogether. Unpinning is easy. However, if the trunk is getting good, you have a great number of pieces on the trunk, and you are still thinking it needs moving around, it may be easier to cut a rough base or backing to mount it on for some quick machine or hand tacking. Do what you need to do to keep moving forward without limiting your ability to make changes or to go with the flow of new ideas. I tend to discourage myself from any stitching until the very end.

Grouping trunks together can be natural and effective. It is interesting how many species merge at the base in some way.

NOTICING LIGHT (VALUE, MOOD)

Some trunks are black silhouettes against light sky. Others have a bit of backlighting or side lighting. Look at pictures and look outside to find the effect you want. If you add lighter (or darker) pieces, just be sure that the new shapes you've made are pleasing. You have positive and negative spaces, perhaps within the same tree trunk and then against the sky. This may affect the perception of width. Use that to your advantage.

No lighting is required for flat-pattern, folkloric, or whimsical styles.

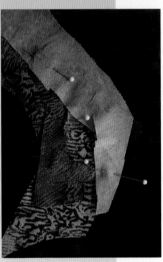

Value check: Trunk against background, as well as new positive and negative shapes

Copper, Bronze, and Gilty Pleasures, 32" x 47", 2002. A densely patterned Art Deco cotton fabric was an unusual choice for trunks, but combined with metallic fabric paint, organza, and a leaf batik, it produced a richly glowing grove of trees in late day.

KNOTS, BURLS, BARK VARIATIONS, AND MOSS (TEXTURE)

This is a time to enjoy the treasures in your scrap bag. Add enriching details with tiny appliquéd pieces. When you begin to look for interesting bark texture you may find knotholes all over your fabric stash. Appliqué the knotholes, letting the rest of the bark flow around them. Or make your own. These little lumpy imperfections can go anywhere you wish to direct the viewer's eye, adding interest while breaking up lines and spaces.

Bark texture can change on one tree. Take advantage of that to use more fabric scraps. Bits of moss may also fit into your plan.

Detail of *Copper Tree*, page 38

QUILTING LINES

Often I refer to the meandering lines of driftwood—the ultimate in quilting possibilities. Your quilting lines can run up and down a living tree, and around the knotholes. Or they can jump back and forth to give the effect of rougher or broken bark. When doing so, your line is giving edges to the bark, making it take on bark shapes.

Making Branches

CHARACTER OF THE TREE OR SHRUB

If you stare at a real branch with twigs, there are many graceful elements to guide you. (And you can cut a window in a piece of paper to peer through and isolate the best elements in your real branch or in tree photos.) You will need to stare carefully to see how branches are formed on the specific tree or shrub you've chosen.

What proportion of your whole piece will need them? And will there be crossing branches, or branches overlapping other trees? (Since you're just pinning, they can go over *or* under.)

CUTTING FABRIC SHAPE

Cut on the bias again. Though you can use smaller versions of your trunk strips, this might be a time to add slightly different colors from your scrap bag. Small bias strips can be folded a bit and tapered on the ends. They will stretch and curve nicely. But if you are doing a corkscrew willow, you will need to cut roundish pieces!

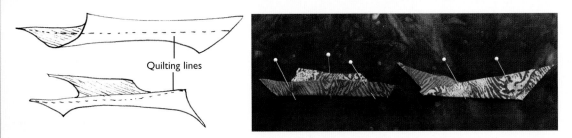

Small bias strips pinned and quilted down for branches

You may like using silk ribbon. It is quite delicate—it folds and twists and then presses neatly.

Old Island Orchard, 37" x 43", 2003. Making an orchard from a large hand-dye involved quilting negative space to leave distant trees puffy. Repetition of silk ribbon trunks assures the viewer that this is indeed an orchard.

Other ribbons also work well. In *Copper Tree,* I used copper-wired ribbon as well as silk ribbon. For this piece, I was lucky to have found a background fabric of delicate branches; so when it came time to make more of them, I found I could work backward with thin ribbon connecting to thicker ribbon and fabric, and ultimately to the tree trunk.

CONNECTIONS

Notice how branches are formed: heavier at the connecting points (nodes), then tapering away.

With each subsequent split, the next branches are smaller. The joints can be interesting, and deserve attention. Think bamboo, with joints. Think calligraphy. Think lumps at the node (see *The Blueberry Bush*). Cutting branches in one piece resembling coral will give a stylized effect that is less natural for trees but that may suit your purposes.

Copper Tree, 26" x 65", 2003. Inspired by a copper-colored discharged cotton and a delicate batik, I added raw silk, silk ribbon, copper-wired ribbon, and yarn.

The Blueberry Bush, 24" x 36", for "Basic Necessities" theme, 2000, private collection, photo by Mark Frey. Something growing is what I need, and I've decided it's a blueberry bush. A little oxygen (I don't take much), some morning dew, a great deal of color (the blueberry bush's specialty), and of course a very good breakfast are my basic necessities.

STITCHING DOWN

The larger branches may need to be appliquéd and quilted randomly afterward. Smaller, more delicate ones can be pinned in place and caught down at quilting time, saving a step. If you are unsure where branches might go, try quilting them onto fine netting, first making several separate small groupings that can be overlapped and arranged at will. Stitching will simply be a matter of fastening the net and trimming it where you don't want it. In *From Walla Walla to Wallula,* I used this technique, with silk and other ribbons on netting.

OTHER OPTIONS FOR BRANCHES

You may use a stamp, either purchased or carved yourself, to repeat branch shapes. You can draw branches or get them from photographs and have photo transfers made. I did both of these in *When Blueberries Aren't Blue* and then added silk ribbons as well, to strengthen the bushes in the foreground.

From Walla Walla to Wallula, 32" x 50", 2003, private collection. Native sagebrush is becoming rare. When I was a child, it seemed to cover the earth.

Detail of *When Blueberries Aren't Blue*

When Blueberries Aren't Blue, 40" x 46", 1999, private collection, photo by Hazel A. Hynds. Rows of blueberry bushes; tiny leaves of vibrant pink, orange, and autumn red blending into a soft rose haze, and the earth underneath sprinkled with fallen leaves.

Making Leaves

CUTTING

Leaves are everywhere in commercial fabric, so finding some appropriate for your trees should be a pleasant search. A printed fabric that pictures leaves overlapping, in a scale that will work for your piece, means that you can cut out chunks and overlay them throughout your branches. But because there is so much variation in how leaves attach to branches, you may have to assemble leaves in clumps or clusters—or the reverse, cut out holes to let in light and air. If your plans require tree leaves against sky, that may be trickier. Solve this fabric selection issue early on. Look for fabrics that have potential sky peeking through, or with leaves against an edge that would blend with sky. You can always color these bits of sky with fabric paint to better blend with the larger sky you've chosen.

Most commercial fabric will need to be turned under to prevent raveling. I've found that batiks do retain a crisp edge. Because I like handwork and portable projects now and then, I've had great fun fussy cutting leaves. You will see me use this process often.

Natural Spot Light, 22" x 57", 2004. This piece uses a repetitive batik for leaves, and copper-wired ribbon to evoke that moment when warm light shimmers on bark.

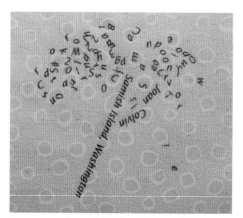

Leaves are just little shapes that cluster.

STIFFENING

For fussy cutting, some spray starch will make leaves easier to deal with. You can decide whether you like to use adhesives of any sort. I don't, because I usually want nothing but the quilting line to touch the surface so the leaf will appear to float. Crisper styles, however, may benefit from actual fusing.

LEAF COLOR

I can lose myself looking up into trees, watching how the light transforms the leaves into different, sparkling colors.

If you can find your leaf fabric in several colorways, go for it. If not, dye part of your fabric in different colors. Or use fabric paint. You will see that I've frequently done this in my work. To do *Vine Maple*, I purchased a leaf stamp for use on antique silk and other fabrics in various colors.

Real maple leaves

Detail of *Vine Maple*, page 59

PLACEMENT OF LEAVES

If you are applying leaves one by one, doesn't it make sense to have that be the last step? I pin on a few, clustering them, to see if I like the effect. If so, I trust that I'll be able to scatter them gracefully later, so I remove them and store them away. It is often much easier to do finish work first, applying the leaves at final quilting time. Remember that branches show through and over leaves. If it is easier to appliqué a portion of a branch on top of leaves, I do just that.

Planting the Tree

How the trunk enters the earth can say lots about the tree's age and environment. Stare at tree bases everywhere. Will the roots show? Have grass or flowers grown up? Is there moss? Are several trees growing in a clump? Are you approaching the tree from the side or from underneath, or are you looking down onto it? Perhaps you see it from behind a small hill?

Selecting from these and a multitude of other situations will help you establish the mood of your piece. Stark, bare, and cold? Meadowlike and welcoming? Flat lowlands or hilly mountain country? Domestic or wild? You see what I mean?

Notice that my piece *Earth Blankets* differs from *Leaf Blankets,* page 43, in that the tree is planted atop a cross section or cutaway slice of the earth's layers. Normal perspective does not apply. That is always an option for you, to evade the necessities that come with realism! In *Leaf Blankets,* the trunks are from a child's perspective—big and buried in the leaves; be sure you don't roll into them.

Earth Blankets, 32" x 54", 2001. This is a strange geology. Picture the continuous blanketing of the soil beneath one special tree. Seasons, years, and centuries . . .

Varying Styles

In *Magic Kingbirds*, I tried a style that was a little more folkloric than usual. The piece needed to be compatible with a Chinese rug. I found a stylized, flat-pattern batik leaf, heavily outlined. And I found bird bodies in some heavily outlined diamond shapes I'd previously painted. Together, these fabrics created a pleasant, whimsical mood that allowed the piece to take on the controlled shape needed to fit a prescribed working space. A stamp replicating one of the fabric leaf clusters let me add leaves in lighter colors.

Leaf Blankets, 41" x 53", 1997, private collection, photo by Hazel A. Hynds. Remember the rich, dizzying smells in the autumn wind, and snuggling down into the earth under piles of dry fall leaves?

Detail of *Magic Kingbirds*

Magic Kingbirds, 72" x 90", 2003, private collection. A colorfully crested imaginary bird watches over his flock.

Potted Tree, 10" x 14", 2004, Janice Coffey, photo by Brett Baunton

Palm II, 10" x 14", 2004, Janice Coffey, photo by Brett Baunton

I think you will enjoy the variations provided by my small study group, a rather diverse set of ladies who enrich my day once a month.

Hazel A. Hynds, known as a quilt historian and for her narrative pieces, has chosen to make a statement using real newsprint to express the spirit of felled trees in *The Sentinel*. The fussy-cut growth is fused flat, rather like a stylized block print, and densely quilted.

Janice Coffey's graphic arts work leads her to make miniature hand-embroidered flat-pattern quilts, and her refreshingly innocent pieces are a thoughtful distillation of shapes cut from her hand-painted fabrics.

Nancy Tupper has had success with liturgical art. She used the mosaic appliqué technique to produce a stylized vertical triptych of essential shapes. Edges are softened with multiple parallel stitching lines.

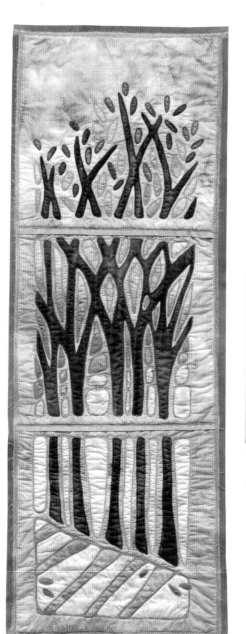

The Sentinel, 20" x 29½", 2004, Hazel A. Hynds. Man vs. nature—the ceaseless demand for commodities

Arbor Triptych, 16" x 44", 2004, Nancy Tupper

6 Add Birds to the Trees (Enlarge Your Subject Matter)

I'm Not a Real Birder

I do try to look carefully, but I'm not a great one for labeling or remembering. Don't be disappointed. I'm learning more and more in spite of myself—watching flight patterns, listening, seeing birds rise up from grasses or swoop down from tall bushes. The tiny little twiggy nest left bare for all to see in winter. I don't catalog, but I store away the visual memory.

When I say, "I'm not interested in recreating a photographic scene, though I could carefully choose fabric to do just that," it means that I'm not sure I really care whether my bird has a median crown stripe, but if I see a dash of white there, in it goes. What I *really* want to do, if I'm honest, is this: juxtapose realism and fantasy only insofar as it intrigues me, with symbolic fabrics to produce summarized forms and suggested texture. I want to be like a child and pick out the good parts, do them with as much skill as I can, and leave out the parts I have no interest in. I want to know enough so that my simple forms breathe a bit, and in so doing cause you to breathe a bit and say, "Oh, yes, it is beautiful out there . . ."

So, the next series of pieces are the result of just these sorts of haphazard relationships with the bird world. I've gotten interested in the colors, the habitat, or the nest structures, and observed enough to be able to recognize when the bird was comfortable in the scene I'd provided for it. That's probably the deciding factor right there. Naturalness.

Feathers and Nests (Texture)

Birds and their nests are soft, round, and texturally diverse. You will see how I've used the softer assembly techniques. I have used commercial fabric in combination with my own hand-painted feathers. But I especially like the technique of combing paint on fabric that I learned from artist Elizabeth Busch. She works freely on artists' canvas, in assorted media. Combing through pigment mixed with a fabric medium, rather like finger painting, produces some fine swirls.

Detail of *Robins*, page 56. The feathers and background are made using fabric combed with paint.

Each of these birds could no doubt have woven its nest faster than I did. Indeed, their clutches would have hatched before my nests were fully composed. It just gives you an added appreciation for nature's ways.

My nests are authentic only in a very rough way. I sometimes wove or crocheted a loose framework, attaching it to branches and later weaving in bits of fabric, strips of raffia, and lichen. If I hesitated over where to put the nest, I made it separately, a luxury birds don't have.

If you think "round," "hollow," and "darker inside," you can weave a nest without a pattern or any more guidance from me. When you have a nest, it can be attached with machine stitching, which will just disappear in the confusion.

Detail of *Finch*, page 49

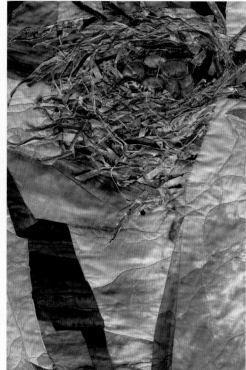

Detail of *Crow*, page 52

Detail of *Cedar Waxwing*, page 50

Bird Studies

Heron

Heron Illusion, 66" x 40", 2003, private collection. When you've watched herons closely in their quiet moments, it is easy to believe they dress as we do, preening and stretching their exquisite wings. Humans call this state of seeing not quite accurately "illusion." Illusion is also the traditional name for the see-through fabrics we use for such moments of finery. Are we not seeing, or are we very much seeing?

Detail

Heron on Beach, 29" x 53", 1995, private collection, photo by Hazel A. Hynds

Heron in Warm Light, 39" x 46", 1997, private collection, photo by Hazel A. Hynds

I've done heron pieces for years. These birds are with me daily, on the beach or in the meadow. Their careful yoga-like movements are calming; the annoyed squawking sound they make when they are disturbed is an almost amusing contrast. You don't expect irritation from a creature so intrinsically splendid.

Antique silk is a natural for the scruffy whiteness of their heads and breasts. And I'm careful to get the heads and beaks painted as authentically as I can—there is a little touch of turquoise beside the eye, and a feathery "chin." Their legs, like everybody's, can be positioned to look their best.

They stand on the tide flats, in tide pools, and on the rocks. The light around them changes the color of every object. Any composition needs to integrate the whiteness of the heads with other light areas. Unrelated white shapes can be distracting or spotty. Here is an opportunity to question whether the viewer's eye can be swirled around a bit, from heads down necks to bodies, or from several heads to a bright patch of water. If you squint, you see that you are making larger, newly shaped blobs of light, which the viewer's eye will delightedly follow.

Finch

My first attempt at a small bird—a sort of finch—was a response to the feathery fabrics I'd been making. When the bird took on life, it was nest-building time. The tree needed to be big to support this body, but not so big that it dominated the composition. By leaving the tree unfinished at the bottom left, I could stay ambiguous about the size of the tree, and the curving diagonal moves the eye in an upward swing. I chose sunny, brushlike sweeps for the background, and many foreground pieces echo that brush stroke. A commercial batik in the wing was repeated and enlarged within the nest.

But that hole in the middle needs help. I didn't spend enough time positioning tree branches. This could and should be corrected.

Let that be a lesson to you.

Finch, 33" x 47", 1999

Vireo

This little bird builds a fancy pouchlike nest. In the West, it is found in live oak trees. I had a densely textured printed batik that could serve as a symbol for their curvy branches and tiny round leaves. It was golden and had a warm pink glow. I carried the gold of the batik across to the nest and the warm pink to the breast of the bird. I matched the pink with a few pink sky openings, so now the batik looked see-through—as if it had been sky all along. The bird is well hidden against the sky; the nest echoes the golden batik.

Getting gnarled old tree branches big enough to set the scale for such a tiny bird was made easier with chunks of decorator fabric. I made a crossing network of branches—more than usual—to encourage the viewer to feel high up in the tree.

Vireo, 44" x 48", 1999, private collection

Cedar Waxwing

I hadn't yet made a cedar tree and it had been on my mind. The *name* of this bird was the hook. My neighbor had just seen one, and I was actively looking.

Exaggerating the color of the bark to get a sunny feel, and exaggerating the yellowness of the bird so he's camouflaged against the trunk established the mood. I used the same bright colors to integrate nest and branches. See those little patterns of orange undersea coral batik? A happy accident as I sorted through my orange stash—the effect of dappled light.

Detail

Cedar Waxwing, 43" x 44", 1999

Should there be sky behind the trunk? No, the dense cedar forests feel deep green, even as light tries to push in. (See the touches of muddy turquoise to let in just a little filtered light?) Part of the point of being a cedar tree is to let off that hypnotic fragrance. Its lacy needles must show so you can smell them as you look. I couldn't find any such fabric, so here again I carved a small block, stamped into thick paint on canvas (using several different green colors), and moved the same block every which way as I stamped—so viewers might be lulled into re-creating the real structure in their heads.

I know. I left out the little red spots on the feather tips. "Red waxy tips on wing feathers are often indistinct and sometimes absent altogether . . ." so the bird books say. But I think about that a lot. I think that if your eye is drawn to an issue more than three times, you need to deal with it. You can fix it, or you can choose to do nothing, as I did in this case.,

Unknown Bird

The architecture of nests got so interesting that I started there. From a cozy center, I literally wove my way outward, circling with tree branches to continue the spiral. And a decorator fabric's rough triangular shapes just gaped open and peeped at me. I had used this fabric quite often but had never seen those triangles as bird mouths—until this nest-building mood overtook me.

So where was the mother? I needed her tail to complete the spiral. Luckily she showed up.

Unknown Bird, 41" x 51", 1999. The circular structure spirals out from the center and inward from the larger branches, so we feel nestled in, yet ready for flight.

Crow

The sleek blackness of the crow and the crevices, the chalkiness of the cliffs, and the warm softness of the nest—a study in contrasts.

I used the *insert* technique to build cliffs using hand-dyes (painting some of them). The bird was cut out whole, from combed fabric. I feel you can do that with a crow; they are so "all of a piece." Note that just the slightest variation in the darkness of the black paint produces some dimension. I did position the crow to lead out from a dark crack, as if he were another dark crevice.

The nest was the softening part. I tipped it a little more than it would really be, to see the bluish eggs (flowers, in a decorator fabric). But tipping works because the cliff is symbolic, not realistic. This is one of my favorite quilts.

Crow, 40" x 50", 1999, private collection. Here my crow is at home in the rocky cliffs, where nests are fit into crevices, and we can feel the angularity of geology juxtaposed with the softness of growing things. We need both.

Corn Stalks with Crow

I continued with stalks because ears of corn were clearly lying in my stash of combed fabrics, in this case muslin. The days seemed like fall.

I also continued the natural weaving scheme in which the verticals arise from the earth and the horizontals intertwine. Over this matrix grow the leaves, a repeated shape. The ears of corn and the bird body further echo this shape. My old crow reflects fading fall sunshine, and dark shadows anchor his shape to the base of the composition.

I'm not sure what he is eating. They were leaves from a different project, but when they were quilted, I'd hoped for corn kernels.

Corn Stalks With Crow, 30" x 60", 2000. There is a bit of sadness and inevitability when fall comes and the earth dries. The crow fits my mood. In dry cornfields, his presence is no longer unwelcome—the fight is over, and his powerful beauty may be accepted without mixed emotions for the moment.

Gull

If you think robins are everywhere, consider seagulls. I've loved them since they first grabbed a cracker from my two-year-old hand.

The idea to do them came as I was matching backgrounds to bird fabrics, thinking "natural habitat." I found a fabric with potential crashing waves, which paired nicely with some Judy Robertson water fabric I'd collected. Together, these fabrics said, "Not on the beach, but way out to sea." And the waves looked bigger, as if you were *above* them. This is called "letting the fabric lead you" and "taking advantage of what you encounter."

I don't know the albatross, or the erne of crossword fame. So seagulls it had to be. I watched them for days, until I could turn them around in my head like an engineer on her computer. Finally, flight seemed possible.

Note that the almost monochromatic color scheme is also a value challenge, mixing light sky and waves with light birds, and mixing shadow into darker water. Here is a sort of vertical yin and yang. Repetition plus size variation is key—bird shapes in decreasing size, and repetition of waves, also becoming smaller to indicate distance.

Gulls, 40" x 47", 2000, private collection. To be at eye level with the gulls or flying with them over tumbling seas would be an awesome experience.

Eagle

We are seeing more and more eagles. This one perches out on a post in the water, watching for ducks. My husband sees him from his office window, and he commissioned—I use the term loosely—a portrait.

My mind was otherwise occupied for too long. When my patron got surly about it, he and the eagle merged in my consciousness, and though the outer dimensions are small, the eagle looms . . .

To be fair, once I started cutting feathers one by one, it got fun. And the flowery shoulder tells you that he's not all that ferocious.

Eagle, 20" x 39", 2000

Robin

So common, yet so beloved.

I'd been saving up red-ochre fabrics (still my favorite color), not knowing where they'd lead. When the mixture of hand-painted pieces began to look like robin breasts, it scared me a little. The robin is an American icon, among the first memories of everyone but the most isolated urbanite.

I knew I would try anyway and that the challenge for me would be to get that quick, perky robin look, and the busy, bustling, get-on-with-it look of spring.

I see them out on the grass—rarely one, but together in groups. Horizontal is good. Lighten the breast color I'd already introduced to a yellowish sunlight color and use the brownish gray of the feathers again in shading or shadows on the grass. Place the robins in clumps, watching where the beaks point in order to develop an overall sort of flattened yin and yang composition. It makes me happy.

Robins, 62" x 29", 1999

Canyon Wren

I found more bird-feather fabrics, really beautiful ones, and they were russet, as was this little wren. So how do I show him with his tiny nest among the huge rocks and crevices that he loves?

Huge rocks. When you haven't this kind of space physically, huge means up close, in the foreground. To break up such a large surface and to use more fabrics, I put in crevices, working back to a sort of grassy lip or overhang of leaves. By now, the rock color was as russet as the bird, so his body was gently hidden. But his white throat would have attracted a predator in a flash, so I added chalky rocks to give him some protection and to integrate white into my scene. (Remember, the eye is drawn to the light values very quickly, so controlling what the viewer sees involves drawing the eye around and about, like a cat following a toy.)

Canyon Wren, 40" x 48", 2000, private collection

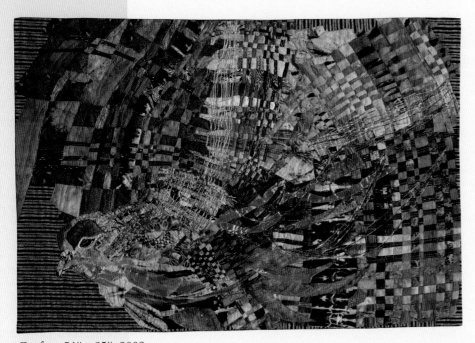

Variation: A Woven Bird

Playing with weaving, I had intended abstraction. Somehow, in assembling chunks of weaving, my lines radiated out, reminding me of a grand tail flourish. Rethinking, I tried couching, wired ribbon, and some appliquéd shapes to get the movement that would sweep the tail outward. A bird head with a very pleased expression finished this experiment.

Fanfare, 51" x 35", 2003

Bodies in Fabric as Subject Matter

Sometimes the subject matter chooses me. I'm following in a long line of would-be artists who couldn't resist the magic of how bodies and flowing fabrics intermingle. It's a formidable group—but I'm pulled in as they were. As I shape the fabric, I'm mentally painting, drawing, and sculpting as well.

I'm always delighted by whose face emerges from the fabric. I wonder what she wants me to say about her. When I begin to know, I simplify the lines and shapes, trying to keep my vision alive and active and to sense where I'm going while I'm stitching. If I leave her for long, her voice might slip away and I'd lose that moment of understanding.

I love relaxed realism if it comes from my inner world—I never set out to recreate a scene. More likely, a face, potential hair, or a gown leads to an explosion of choices and ideas that sort themselves out randomly, happily, and with no observable pattern until the end, when I too am surprised by who she is and what she is doing.

Fabric is a good symbol for women, beginning with the earliest spinners and weavers. Fabric is of the earth; the connection is there. Fabric is part of living, growing, and nurturing. It accompanies women who are responding, wondering, looking for strength, finding direction, caring about, and caring for. Feet on the ground, or arm around the tree, solutions to these yearnings and reflections come easier outside.

What I've been saying to you explains my subject matter. It demonstrates my passion and commitment to it. And the short explanation below each of the pieces that follow—the "art statement" for the public—is another way I share intent and perhaps guide the viewer.

All other text you will read in this section is quite different. It will be a bit like going backstage . . . Any magic seems a miracle after you glimpse the chaos behind the curtain. I'm serious. You may wish to stop here.

Detail of *Baltic Retro*, page 66

Backstage

Integrating Body Into Background

Putting a figure in a setting of any sort is a major design issue. Classical portrait painters were very unsubtle about this—they showed you with your favorite dog, your musical instruments, all your hobbies laid out around you. Many chose to put you on a bench in the garden, if you were lucky.

Generally, I'd like my figures in better connection with the earth. I'm not quite comfortable making their forms morph into tree trunks, but I think leaning against one for strength is fair enough. Placing the body in a relationship with the background helps me understand who this person is. What I'm suggesting is that all we know about good design must help us choose agreeable positions and repetition in forms, if applicable, using lines and shapes that lead and direct the viewer's eye.

Vine Maple, 38" x 56", 2002, private collection. A wide range of colors and little variation in value keep this grove of maples vibrant yet serene—a place in which to spend some quiet time.

Issues of depth and perspective will come up as you decide your stylistic approach and see what sort of portraiture is possible. Flat figures with little definition of features can fly about your "canvas," needing no anchoring and no attention to classical rules of drawing. You will see in the following pieces that I pick and choose from the rules at will.

Value, however, is always an issue, whatever style you are using. It is of particular importance when working with figures. The world has become enchanted with Vermeer because he lit his faces from without and from within. Light-valued faces connect with necks and bodices and arms and aprons and jewelry, flowing around and about, meshing and merging with dark shadows in clothing and dark furniture. Even if you are working more abstractly with much simpler or flatter figures, you won't want to miss opportunities to use the drama of value. Do whatever is needed to evaluate the relationships among your lights and darks—instant photography, black-and-white photocopying, tiny quick sketches of what you see, squinting. As you work, you can't do this too often.

Detail

Cave Drawn, 28" x 62", 2002, private collection. She is drawn into the darkness for reconnection with the earth. The dark is welcoming, offering sanctuary, solace, breathing space, and a place for strengthening of purpose. Inside the cave, will she become someone else?

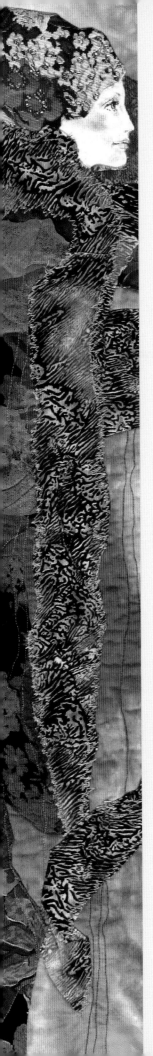

Making Faces

If you are comfortable with portraiture, you will also be inventive with how to produce it. I can tell you what I have done. I press very fine muslin onto freezer paper for stability. Then, using pencils, colored pencils, and pastel pencils, I begin shading. As I become more sure, I darken, ending with Pigma pens. I make several faces at a time, and throw lots away. The slightest jog of a pencil or pen may ruin the whole thing. Those that have potential, I press to set, then spray lightly with a moisture repellent such as 3M's Scotchgard. (Practice, of course.)

I do not contour the outer edge of the face, nor do I determine where the neck connects, preferring to do that at the last minute as I turn edges under for appliquéing. To help keep the face from wrinkling grotesquely and to provide an opacity that hides the seam allowance, sandwich Steam-A-Seam between the face fabric and a piece of muslin. Cut both the Steam-A-Seam and the muslin to the exact shape of the head, pressing them onto the back of the face fabric, which stays untrimmed until it's time to turn under for appliquéing. This way the face isn't stuck onto the batting by the ironing process and will then move freely, further reducing the chance of wrinkling.

I caution you to photograph faces before and after application. Before you stabilize the face, a photo will tell you immediately whether the contours are pleasing, whether a few corrections in value are possible if needed, or whether any facial elements are hopelessly out of alignment. Even a usable face will need to be pinned into place while you are still in the composing process, so color and value can be balanced, either by adding color or shadows to the face or by modifying the background intensities to best display the face you've made. At this time, you can fold fabric loosely to play with various neck positions. Photography at this stage will help you see what is, not what you hope and assume. After you've applied the face to the quilt, rephotograph. Appliqué stitches may need to be more delicate, or the face piece may need to be pulled more taut to smooth out wrinkles.

This technique, I think, is successful only with very small faces, 2" to 4" high. Beyond that, you move into more complex surface dimension and textural issues. Recently, I've been delighted with improvements in the photo-transfer process. Not only can I get black and white, and living color, but can also choose one of hundreds of single colors. This has meant that I needn't always draw my faces on muslin (nor do I need the protective spray), but can do my drawing on paper. With photo-transfer processes, our choices widen—multiple images, reversed images, enlargements within reason, not to mention the application of image to various colors and textures of fabric. Those of you who aren't comfortable drawing faces yourselves will be equally attracted to this process because you can reproduce (with permission!) photos and art from many sources. Read current literature and experiment. Take classes in drawing figures and faces.

Variation

In *Who Are We This Time?* I have used a decidedly different style (hard-edge, traditional strip piecing) to produce a mirrored image look. The face of the girl with long red hair is drawn on fabric; all other faces are various photo transfers of that original face.

Who Are We This Time? 41" x 54", 1998. Try to find yourself in a click-on, try-on, mood- and mind-changing magic mirror.

Detail of *Woman with Madrona*. Hair and leaves mesh around this enigmatic woman.

Hair

My design concept from the beginning has been to find "hair" that emerges from the texture of the background fabric. I'm happiest when it is integrated into the background in some way—through ambiguity of color or shape. I try to find highlights within the fabric. See detail of *Woman with Madrona* and *Women of the Cloth*.

Women of the Cloth, 48" x 58", 1996, private collection. Women who do good work must walk a special path. To emphasize such timeless efforts, I chose garments that might appear in any era.

In *Vine Maple* (page 59), I used so much metallic paint in the leaves that I needed to balance and integrate the figure by continuing to use it to highlight the hair.

Sometimes I will appliqué an extra piece of hair fabric to soften a face, but rarely do I touch the outer edge. That's just the style choice I've made. Quilting lines also provide growth direction, texture, and highlights. Extra threadwork can be useful, as in *Flowers of the Mainau* and *Night Vision*.

Flowers of the Mainau, 44" x 53", 1998, private collection, photo by Hazel A. Hynds. Picking armloads of wild flowers . . . indeed a fantasy most anywhere.

Night Vision, 43" x 47", 1997. I am struck by the beauty of the night—at first colorless, but after reflection fully vibrant within a subdued palette. The details of night objects are unlocked and unleashed by the intensity of our need to see. We know who she is and why she sits there, for we all have our moments of night vision.

Gowns

The costume room—oh, my . . . Endless yards of rich, flowing colors and textures, wherein live the ghosts of all great seamstresses. *Baltic Retro* is a gathering of gowned theater people, perhaps.

It's fun to experiment with what fabric can do in costumes that painters have to imitate. Some classicists were so anxious to get the shine and pattern of the brocade that their human models emerged less interesting by comparison. As I said before, fabric is symbolic to us—rough cotton and a little real lace for the pioneer *Great Aunt Jenny* and antique silk for the undergarment in *One More Sunrise*. We have an enormous symbolic language from which to make our points.

Baltic Retro, 44" x 44", 1998. Sometimes I express sadness by returning to beauty and elegance that are no longer. Perhaps, though, these are theater people, at peace while they are protected by warm, colored lights.

Detail of *One More Sunrise*, private collection, photo by Hazel A. Hynds. I like this woman and want to ask her why she sits there. What is on her mind? What will she do next? Sometimes I think I know what I meant for her and then it eludes me . . .

"Does your daughter know you are making only the front of her wedding gown?" (Comment in class from a clever student.)

It is a luxury to do just the parts that show. The fun for me is to get all the flowing lines as simply as I can. (Please see *Eve in the Northwest*, page 68) Take a tiny tuck here and there. Work on the bias. As you would experiment with different ways to tie a scarf, experiment with various folds and dress lines. Tack down invisibly by hand, unless you see stitching lines that define or emphasize the look. Be sure to notice shapes behind sheers or other transparent fabrics, and use them to advantage. (I've learned to press my dress fabrics before I spend time draping and pinning.)

Great Aunt Jenny, 32" x 55", 2001, private collection. My mother remembers her aunt Jenny as having a wild tangle of red hair and an adventurous spirit. She came West to stake a claim, to begin farming. We have her small steamer trunk, a few pieces of lace, and little else.

Eve in the Northwest,
44" x 53", 2002.
Because it was the most
beautiful place I knew
in my childhood vision,
Eve is walking through
the woods of the
Northwest. Whatever
she encountered, she
found among the cedar,
vine maple, and
huckleberries.

Scenery: Backdrop for Your Figure

As I've said, basic to my own work is relating figure to background, and I often wrestle with these relationships. (I'm thinking of doing some pieces in which figures appear on stark monochromatic backgrounds for a change of mood and style.)

In finding the setting for my figure, I've found it helpful to temporarily consider the figure a separate entity. As she takes form, and ideas for her relationship to the world also take form, I can manipulate the figure, just as I do in making tree trunks. (Pin her together as we did the tree trunk, or put her on a base, page 34.) If hair is a part of the background, recognize that you can probably tweak that fabric around on your design wall as you are finding the best placement for the figure. You may be surprised by a totally new idea as the figure interacts with other fabrics, so stay open and let yourself be led along. During the making of *Great Aunt Jenny* (page 67), I took successive snapshots, cutting apart the photos instead of physically manipulating the real fabric.

Use any or all of the techniques presented in earlier chapters to build banks of flowers, drifts of shrubbery, or groves of trees. Or if you are working like Matisse or Klee, enjoy relating shapes, colors, and values as forms fly about.

You Are the Director

The entire costume room is available to you, an eclectic assortment of actors and actresses awaits you, and you are in control of the script, the lighting, the sets, and the length of the action. Plus, as the director, you can choose your approach—hard edge, soft and gentle, realistic or mystical, with any personal touches you wish to add.

You will have a hit, I'm sure.

Some Last-Minute Details

Embellishment

I often say to myself, "That's a last-minute detail." Apparently this means to me that I know it's coming, but I don't yet need to decide because it doesn't affect my design or other decisions. A perfect example of such a delayed detail is the application of real feathers (or metal, buttons, ornaments, or other embellishments). These objects can be fragile and/or cumbersome. True, they take up space, and their edges become lines. So you prepare for their presence either with dummy shapes or with clear knowledge of their effect.

Feathers are my favorite, though. In the following pieces you'll see marabou, seagull, and duck feathers. (If I've gathered them myself, a couple of minutes in the microwave will sanitize them.) I fasten with thread, and sometimes a bit of glue. In *Waiting in the Wings*, the dark splotches of dye already looked furlike,

Detail of *Waiting in the Wings,* private collection; photo by Hazel A. Hynds. A vibrant hand-dyed fabric needs only the glamour of marabou and beads to evoke those moments before the curtain rises.

but marabou was nice around the faces. In *Children of Bolivia,* the marabou helped make shiny black hair.

Children of Bolivia, 35" x 49", 1998, private collection. for Ann Miletich's humanitarian project. A quilter's salute to the awayo, which Bolivian mothers weave to hug and carry their children.

In *Vessel*, I made tiny pockets for the gull feathers, so they could be removed for protection.

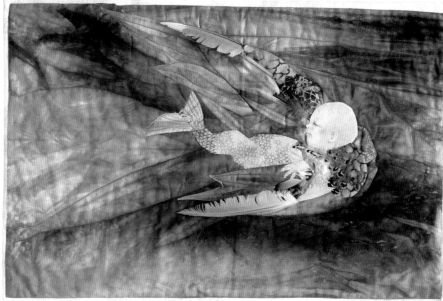

...his own dear body is as sturdy a vessel as soul could hope to sail in...

Vessel, 33" x 24", 2000. Based on a quotation from Sena Naslund's *Ahab's Wife*, this newborn unites air, water, and earth, using real gull and duck feathers.

Framing: What You Do With the Outer Edges

Opening Night, 40" x 42", 2001, private collection. You can see in the distance the sparkling lights of an infinite audience. Yet there are the empty velvet seats over the black hole of anonymity. Which will it be?

Framing, too, seems a last-minute thing. Yes and no.

I'm torn between two realities. The art quilt theory is that the frame (or border, or binding, or whatever) is part of your composition and, as such, may not even be needed. That surely makes sense. The other is a certain awe at how you can take a picture to the framer and receive it back looking as if it would be comfortable in the Metropolitan.

This means that I always rather dread the moments when framing decisions must be made. About three-quarters of the way through my working process—when I begin to know where my outer edges will be (and can still do something about them)—I mull over what my piece needs. Should the visual action continue outward freely, not stopped by framing? I see some of my work as snapshots of the outdoors, and in those I have used only the tiniest of edges.

Or, might the action be stopped and focused in some way to make a point? For example, *Great Aunt Jenny* (page 67) leans against the barn, and theater people are poised above the gilded stage apron in *Opening Night*.

Perhaps framing is a chance to strengthen a symbol? I used a giant symbolic feather to frame *Observing Wild Swans* (a Judy Robertson fabric, of course).

Look back at *Baltic Retro* (page 66) and notice that the frame is reminiscent of the Art Deco period.

You are on your own here, my friends. You'll need to see what style you've used, ask yourself what the frame is meant to do, and then search to see the millions of compatible choices before you.

Observing Wild Swans, 38" x 58", 1996, private collection. No matter who you are, your breath stops for the few moments you watch swans in flight. I like it that people from ancient lands have seen them too— a shared moment, quite timeless.

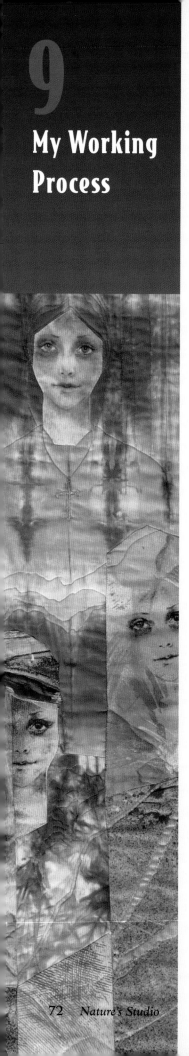

9

My Working Process

This chapter should be read only when you are ready for some specific information and know how to use it. I've put off discussing my personal working process because I want you to think through your own. But now I can do it in the hope that it will help you devise or refine a process for yourself. Your process needs to provide useful continuity for you on your best days, and to carry you along on days when moments of trepidation might derail you. Look honestly at your objectives first.

Making the Process Fit Your Needs

What I'm looking for in a working process is freedom. The process I've come to treasure is the freest I know, the most open to possibilities, and the most unlimited by rules. If I have a plan, fine. If I don't, fine. Somewhere in a pleasant, haphazard collection of fabrics, an idea for them will grab me and won't let me go. There is no proscribed starting place, and I can go forward, backward, over, and on top—both in creating and in assembling.

I like this system, too, because I am happiest working fast and with intensity. I glimpse an idea, and I can't wait to see it done. How will it all come out? I've taught myself to juggle all the elements so I can chase the image while I know where it might go, and while I still care!

I can sustain this kind of focused energy for about three consecutive days, which is also about all the time I feel I can carve out from normal family obligations. This is usually almost enough for the creative effort; then the engineering can proceed at a leisurely pace.

Here's My Procedure

Preliminary Idea or Vision

From various sources come a possible design, possible colors, possible size. I pose questions for the subconscious, living with the idea.

Immerse in the Subject

I find out what I might need to know through research, photos, and observations, until I have much more information than I will need—enough so it feels like it is spilling over.

Audition Fabric

I spread my selections around in piles, intuitively using larger amounts of some, smaller amounts of others. I reject textures and patterns not compatible with the mood and flavor I'm planning. I pick out the most likely of all these fabrics, pinning them up on the design wall. Then it's time for instant photographs, to see how they interact. (Some hand-dyes take on an overpowering three-dimensional look.) There may or may not be a keynote fabric.

"Aha!" Response

I wait for some connections in the fabric that jolt me. There has to be a little electricity to make this interesting. I keep manipulating until it comes.

Serious Preliminary

I decide that I'm ready to explore. I prepare my "canvas" of backing with batting on top, and smooth it onto the design wall. Since size is usually unknown at this point, I often start with a 2-yard piece (45" wide) of backing that starts as high as I can comfortably reach and drapes onto the ground. (I'm looking at the wrong side of the backing. Later I will trim it off and will no doubt have enough left for casings or hanging sleeves.) Then I spread the batting (Cotton Classic, or similar) over the backing, using sticky notes on the leftover pieces to remind myself which is length and which is width. Pieces will hang better if the batting grain direction matches the backing grain direction.

I press some possible backgrounds and apply them to my design wall. I sort out categories of fabric by color, by texture, or by where I might want to use them—whatever makes sense. I think about possible assembly techniques, but I don't have to decide yet.

Work for Real

This is the time I need to be alone, or at least focused. I go into robot mode around the house.

I try to work for real, picking the best parts of the fabric, rough cutting the design elements. (Either I leave extra, or I plan to recut or add some things, so I'm not at all worried about whether I have the right shape; I just want a hunk of the fabric in a shape that I can manipulate.) I pin, staying flexible. "This is what I think I want to do . . . We'll see." I try to stay light on my feet, playing a little haphazardly with the design elements.

When the space is filled, I stand back, thinking about the effect. This is an important part for me in that I'm testing my conviction. As I stand back, I'm seeing what needs to be rearranged or changed. I may feel the need to clean the slate, get a fresh start, clear away the underbrush. But sometimes the rough "brush stroke" is powerful as it is now pinned. So I'm wavering: "I know I can get this piece back on at least as well as it is now, maybe better." Or, "I'll never equal this . . . Leave it alone." Luckily, with the pinning process, I can remove some objects intact, to later rearrange, but I won't have to *re-form* them; that's been done.

Now I'm restarted, making changes in the design, enriching patterns and colors.

Assess

Throughout this last step, I've been using the instant camera and my reducing glass. I'm still learning to ask the right questions, to zero in on the trouble spots. If I can identify an issue, there are numerous ways to solve it. The assessing process goes on at frequent intervals as I stand back to look.

Prepare for Stitching

When it all seems the best I can do at the moment, I feel ready to take it off the wall for machine appliquéing. By sliding my hand behind the backing, I can reposition pins to go through all the layers, adding pins as needed to keep the fabric from shifting. The sandwich is sufficiently secure to move to the table surface. I check to be sure I haven't pinned wrinkles into the backing. Now I re-pin an inch or so apart, perpendicular to the stitching line, so I will be able to machine stitch easily over the pins or remove them as I go. I don't baste, because sometimes I want to ease or stretch or change a line as it occurs to me when stitching.

As I pin, I turn some raw edges under, and I leave some rough. I place inserts where batting shows through. These are design issues that may change the look, so when it's all pinned, I lift it back onto the design wall for more assessment. Too neat? Too stiff? Lots more tweaking to be done.

Stitch

When I feel ready to stitch, I roll the piece from the ends or top to isolate the area I'm going to work on. Generally, I stitch outward from the center to the edges, as we've been taught. (Any rippling will occur only at these outside edges.) If there is a choice, I work the vertical grain first—less chance of stretching. I use a tiny zigzag stitch that neatly appliqués hard edges, and I move inside a quarter-inch or so to be sure any soft edges are anchored. I prefer clear monofilament for the needle, and cotton quilting thread for the bobbin. I am intent upon appliquéing the shapes down, thinking, however, that many places won't need it and can remain pinned until quilting time. This is a fast process that suits my need to get things fastened so I can see the piece on the wall again for corrections and details.

Because I expect to make corrections as part of this process, I leave threads hanging loose. Later, after the appliquéing, I will, as pleasant handwork, pull the top thread to the back and bury both, using a self-threading notched needle. I just pop the two threads through the notch and run the needle into the batting. Tiny, short ends can be done this way since you can bury the needle first. I bury all the appliqué stitching at this point, so there will be no threads to tangle in the quilting process.

Corrections

Stitching tightens things up. I allow time now to rip and re-pin here and there, to appliqué new shapes where softening might be needed, and to generally make design corrections. A good time to consider framing is while the piece is on the wall.

Framing

Now I'm thinking about the character of the outer edges—any framing needs to be integrated with what is happening in the piece. Measuring is appropriate now, if I want to square up or ensure flatness.

Final Appliqué

I finish stitching any appliqué corrections and tentatively stitch any frame elements integral to the piece, realizing that the quilting process may ripple the edges and require changes in the frame.

Quilting

I work from the center out to the edges. I don't go all the way to the edge if I think the edge fabrics will need tightening up or repositioning. When the quilting is all done except for the edges, I steam the quilt flat and do any re-pinning, measuring, or adjusting that's needed. Last-minute appliquéing and quilting are done just before the binding is applied.

Add Any Fragile Embellishments

Apply binding, add any fragile embellishments, label, and make casings or other devices for hanging.

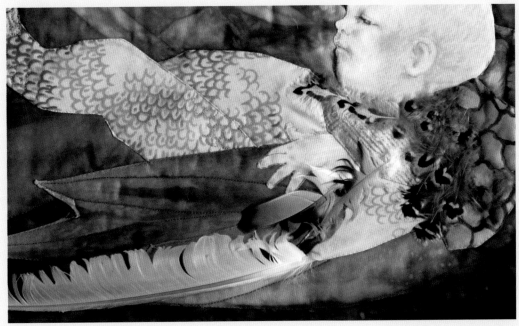

Detail of *Vessel*, page 70

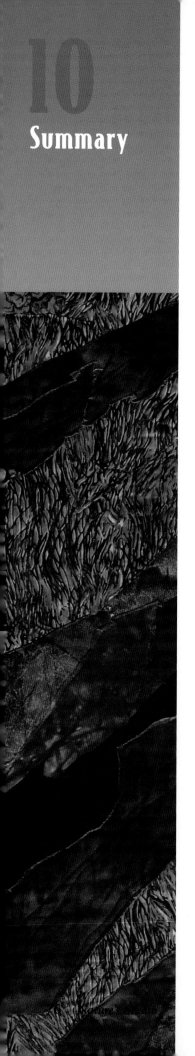

I'm hoping that by taking apart the process by which art is attempted, and by touching on some of the components of design, you will better see what all art has in common. I hope to have shown you some of what all fabric artists have in common. I hope you will now have a richer concept of what sort of divergence is possible, rejoicing in how extremely different we can be within the fiber-art family.

Finding Your Truth

No matter what medium, what approach, there will be work that lives and work that doesn't. Your chances of creating work in the first category are better if your choices come together to express something personal, something about which you care. How do you sort out the details of living?

I amuse myself with the issue of detail. If I'm writing, I ask, "How much do you want to know?" or if I'm cleaning my house, "How far back into the corners today?" Each morning's newspaper poses issues of detail. Photography is so good; these sorts of things might catch your eye:

- A familiar building, but by moonlight you see it differently
- A common bird, enlarged so you can almost see hand stitching around the eye
- Fields, tidelands seen from the sky; complex flat patterns like old paisley fabrics

And sometimes the graphics are astounding. Swift brush strokes to wash color or illustrate a lead story with flavor and vigor. The good ones tell you in color and line what you will want to begin to read. Don't you love how the essence is clear in the simplest cartoons? That's what brings up your laughter—finding those truths in tiny details that make the cartoonist's point, leaving out everything else.

So it is always a pleasant push-pull, this issue of detail. Shall we use *many* (for richness, for pattern, for accuracy), or shall we use *few* (for speedy understanding, for focus, for power, for humor)?

These are the sorts of musings that help you understand yourself and help you focus on what you care about. You and your friends look at the same thing and see it differently. I suppose the real difference is that each of us has internalized symbols for what might be natural, unusual, or useful to make a statement. Such an open field! What are the details that you see?

Knowing the Material You Choose to Use for Art

Whether your medium is leather, metal, or a textile, when you are ready to work, it is less frustrating if you understand how it behaves—how it cuts or spreads, how it reflects light, how and if it bends or curves, how it interacts or mixes with other substances. This knowledge of your material absorbs you sleeping or waking and vibrates in your fingertips as you think what you can do with it and what you can help it to say, coaxing out its best qualities. You are literally compelled to get your fingers into it.

Control, Balance, and Focus (Lovely Words)

My sister reminded me that I was intent upon coloring inside the lines for many years. "You were learning what control was all about," she said. Now, I guess I'm working hard to make sure that a messy stroke is messy in a pleasing way. My heroes are the Asian painters who lived a lifetime learning to make 30 perfect brush marks in 30 perfect places. They learned control, balance, and focus. Wouldn't we love to have those as life skills? Dark days and light days. Things you have to do, things you want to do. Large in your life, small in the scheme of things . . .

Uncertainties

But nobody is immune from insecurities. If you have too many in your life, choose a working style that gives you comforting control and a predictably pleasant result. Use fabric the way you need to. But do not let the use of fabric be part of any insecurity. That is, plan to direct your own work. See what you need and figure out how to get it. If you can easily learn from others, read or take classes; if not, improvise. I call this creative problem solving, because invention comes out of a search for solutions. So let the way you choose to work satisfy your personal needs.

You may have a comfortable working process, but there are sure to be moments of uncertainty within it. I hope you will learn to observe and sense your degree of conviction. How far ahead do you need to see? How far ahead into the implementation? Can you trust yourself to get there? Answers to these questions will help you choose working methods that fit.

Put another way, listen as your inner voice is mumbling. At different times, you will hear: "I know what I want here; I have several thoughts on how to do it." Fine. Or, "I'm pretty sure I can make this happen, so I'll go on." Fine, too. Or, "I haven't a clue what to do here. I'd better go look at . . . or rethink . . . or change . . ." Also fine. Just recognize that if having a very long leash makes you uncomfortable, shorten it and make some simpler rules for your working style. But let me assure you, with each piece you do, your voice will become more authoritative and more convincing—both to yourself and to your viewers.

I think it is completely normal to be uncertain much of the time. There is a difference, though, between *uncertain* and *floundering*. I never feel I am floundering because I have learned to identify what is happening: I may be tired. I may be annoyed that I've made unsuccessful choices. I may recognize that I have a bad idea. These sorts of things you can deal with. You accept that the creative process will have ups and downs and will not always be comfortable.

No matter how secure you feel about your work, there will come a point when you are satiated with it and can no longer make effective judgments. You need fresh eyes. Asking a friend for advice can be helpful, but don't let this become a quagmire. Getting good critiquing takes some practice in both asking and telling. Some advice:

- Just as personnel directors talk to "observable behavior" and not to whether you are a good or bad person, you will need to hear what your friend *observes* going on in your piece. What might she see that you didn't? Are her observations meshing with your intent? Are any areas confusing to her? Now that is helpful information.

- Don't work for her (or anyone else's) approval. "I wonder if she'll like it now?" is not a healthy approach, is it? You've given up responsibility; it is no longer yours.

If another person isn't available when you need help, try taking your piece into a neutral room—say, the kitchen—and looking at it out of the corner of your eye. Or look at it in the mirror. See if you can articulate the problem areas by posing questions to yourself, and then go get some sleep.

Revelation comes when you are least expecting it—while the dog is scratching in the middle of the night or when you are pouring orange juice. Just don't be surprised if at the lowest moment, when you've begun to think you've wasted your time totally, your brain will offer a suggestion. The creative part of your brain hasn't given up as quickly as you have, and it can set you on the right track. Soon all the pent-up frustration will seem to pour out; you will watch decisions flowing easily and your fingers working deftly. Count on it.

In Summing It All Up, Dear Friends . . .

My definitions and explanations have come from my own experiences. They are abbreviated as well as debatable! But they will serve as guidance and as clues to where more detailed study might be useful.

This is how I see it: The hugest part of making art of any kind is the result of a passion or desire to have it happen. Intense caring. Please understand me when I say this intensity does not assume a complicated result. You can be intensely occupied and caring while you plan a nine-patch or a small abstraction. Your desire to speak through an art medium has little to do with the complexity of your plans. You just need the momentum that comes from a huge desire to make something happen.

Next come the choices reflecting how you want it to look. Choose your way of putting lines and shapes together. My choices are soft edge and semi-realism. You can read elsewhere for thorough discussions of hard edge and geometry. There is enormous room for combinations between these two extremes. So you are choosing what might be called the character or style that will best express your ideas.

Now it's time to sew, to assemble. Notice that some kinds of assembly require the same sort of creative emotional effort used in the design phase. Other kinds are less exhausting. Choosing how to carry out your plans is part of your style.

Your piece results from these three stages. I hope I have been able to break down some of the things you need to know into manageable chunks. It is hard to be orderly. You need to get an overview in one big gulp so you can see the implications.

Finding your style is finding your way of putting lines and shapes together to say something. It's developing a working procedure that supports you so you can move forward smoothly. It's moving back and forth physically to see the piece from all distances, and it's moving in and out mentally to absorb its details as well as its total impact. It's seeing your piece as a whole—all the parts relating and moving together into one big experience for the eye.

I wish for you the joy of discovery, the release of emotions that comes from sharing, and a lifetime with this tantalizing substance—fabric.

With love,

Joan

Index

About the Author

In 1988, after pursuing an assortment of careers and bringing up her family in Southern California, Joan Colvin began her career in quiltmaking. Since discovering that her two loves, art and fabric, could be united, she has been a studio quilt artist, author, lecturer, and teacher.

Returning to the Northwest influenced her choice of subject matter and color. The Colvin home in the San Juan Islands overlooks Puget Sound, with its seasonal assortment of flying wildlife.

My small study group (see their quilts on page 44): Hazel A. Hynds, Janice Coffey, and Nancy Tupper; photo by Ted Mains